Behind the Scenes

MUSIC

JUDITH ANDERSON

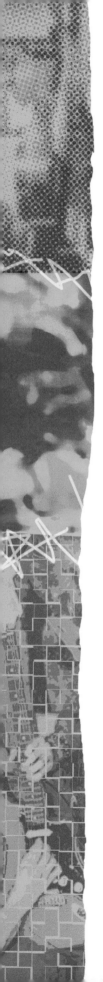

First published in 2009 by Wayland

Wayland
338 Euston Road
London NW1 3BH

Wayland Australia
Level 17/ 207 Kent Street
Sydney NSW 2000

Editor: Nicola Edwards
Design manager: Paul Cherrill
Designer: Rita Storey

British Library Cataloguing in Publication Data

Anderson, Judith, 1965-
Music. - (Behind the scenes)
1. Music - Vocational guidance - Juvenile literature
2. Music trade - Vocational guidance - Juvenile literature
I. Title
780.2'3

ISBN: 978-0-7502-5890-6

The author and publisher would like to thank the following for permission to reproduce quotations
in this book: p12 BBC Online; p13 *The Independent*; p19 (t) *The Guardian*; p19(b) Monster; p22
The Irish News; p23 TheSite.org; p25 *Observer Music Monthly*.

The author and publisher would like to thank the following for permission to reproduce the
following photographs in this book:
© Everynight Images/Alamy p18, © Joel Wintermantle/Alamy p9, Justin Kase ztwoz/
Alamy p27, © Lebrecht Music and Arts Photo Library/Alamy pp15 and 20, © Trinity
Mirror/Mirrorpix/Alamy pp14 and 25; i-stock cover and pp1, 2, 7, 8, 16, 23, and 24;
Jo Hale/Getty Images pp19 and 26, John Shearer/WireImage/Getty p21, Matt Cardy/Getty
Images p12, Mat Szwajkos/Getty Images p28; Shutterstock p5; Tudor Photography 4, 6, 11,
22 and 30.

Printed in China

Wayland is a division of Hachette Children's Books,
an Hachette UK company.
www.hachette.co.uk

Contents

Why music?

Are you thinking about a job in music? The music industry employs tens of thousands of people in the UK. Some of these people are musicians, singers, songwriters or composers – people who 'make' music. Others are producers and sound engineers, promoters and record label executives, DJs and press officers. The range of careers is huge, yet everyone is united by a single passion – music.

A competitive industry

The music industry is a highly competitive area of work. This is because lots of people want to work in a creative and stimulating environment with music at its heart.

Many people who now earn their living working in the music industry will tell you that they started out by working for free, on a work placement or as a volunteer in order to gain vital experience and demonstrate their commitment to future employers.

↓ *Listening to music, researching it and developing opinions about it are the first steps towards a future career in the industry.*

An unpredictable industry

Many music professionals are self-employed. This means they work on a short-term basis, sometimes hiring out their skills for a single concert or event. This gives them more freedom to decide what they want to do, and when. It also means they don't have the security of a regular job or steady income. Almost all jobs in music involve long hours and a constantly changing routine.

A changing industry

The music industry never stands still. Not only do jobs come and go, but the way music is made, produced, marketed and sold is going through a period of rapid change. This is partly due to new developments in technology. Digital media is transforming the way music reaches its audience. Ten years ago, no one had heard of 'downloading' music!

About this book

This book provides an overview of careers in music by looking at the jobs people do. As well as examining skills, experience and qualifications it reveals some of the challenges associated with working in music and answers questions about how to break into this exciting and demanding industry.

↑ *Working in music can be challenging and unpredictable. You need to be passionate about what you do.*

Any questions

Do you need qualifications to make it in music?

Qualifications depend on what it is you want to do. If you want to teach music, for example, you will almost certainly need a teaching qualification. A business degree might be useful if you want to run a record company. However, qualifications are not essential for many jobs in music. What matters most is that you show talent and commitment, you understand how the industry works and you are prepared to put music first. Excellent communication skills are vital in every job, whether you are playing in an orchestra, managing a band or writing a press release. IT skills are important too.

Making music

Hip hop or chamber music? Pop or opera? Rock or jazz? Music is a wonderfully diverse art form, delivered to us in a wide variety of ways. Whether it's a new album or an advertising jingle, a busker on the street or a West End musical, music is all around us. Composers and musicians are constantly striving to create the very best sounds for us to enjoy.

A working life

Musicians work hard to bring their music to an audience. Performance is only a small part of the daily or weekly routine.

Even though many will have gone through a rigorous musical training, musicians never stop rehearsing, practising and improving. Then there are auditions to attend, agents and bookers to call, sound checks to carry out and promotional tasks such as posting leaflets and updating websites to consider. Travelling can take up a great deal of time, too, especially when on tour.

Fame and fortune?

We all know about the musicians who make it to the 'big time', playing to huge audiences and selling albums in record-breaking quantities. But most composers, songwriters, instrumentalists and singers don't achieve this level of commercial success. Few have permanent jobs, and even members of an opera company or an orchestra are likely to be on a short-term contract that lasts for no more than a year or two.

This singer is working with a voice coach to improve her technique in preparation for the next audition.

Often musicians are paid per song or per performance. It can be an unstable way to earn a living and many have additional non-music jobs in order to pay the bills.

Session musicians

Nevertheless, there are all sorts of jobs such as being a session musician, a backing singer or writing music for advertising, computer games, film and TV that allow musicians to spread the risk and earn steadily by working on a range of different projects. Session musicians are hired by the day or even by the hour to accompany solo artists who don't have a band, play an instrument that the band members can't play, record music for advertising jingles or play at promotional events. A good session musician will be able to read music and get it right first time – producers won't pay for you to practise!

THINKING AHEAD

As with all creative jobs, establishing yourself as a singer, a musician, a songwriter or composer requires talent and commitment.

• Get as much experience as you can, performing for free in venues such as schools in order to hone your skills.

• Sing in a choir or join an orchestra or youth band – even if this isn't what you want to do in the long term it will provide you with invaluable training and experience.

• If you want to write songs or compose, get friends to perform your compositions as you'll learn a lot from the way others interpret your work.

• Learn to read music – this is especially important if you want to work as a session musician or in an orchestra.

Teaching and music therapy

Not all musicians and music-makers want to make a career out of public performance. Some people prefer to use their skills to help others learn and experience the pleasure of music-making for themselves.

Teaching music

You love music, and you know a lot about it. Perhaps you play a couple of instruments or sing or compose. Well, teaching music is a wonderful way to combine your passion and talent for music with a satisfying and rewarding career. Remember, however, that teaching requires its own set of skills.

Do you enjoy working with people? Are you patient, flexible, a good listener and communicator? And are you prepared to learn yourself?

Qualifications

Music teachers must be able to read music and play at least one instrument to a very high standard. They usually have formal musical training to degree or conservatoire level. If they want to teach in schools they will also need a teaching qualification from a college or university. Music teachers who work for private clients don't always have degrees but they will usually have some kind of teaching qualification from a recognised professional organisation.

Music therapy

A music therapist uses music to help clients deal with physical, emotional and mental problems, such as stress, eating disorders, language difficulties or disability.

→

Music teachers help students to develop their musical abilities.

↑ *Music therapists help clients to express themselves and to have fun through music.*

A music therapist is not a teacher, and the aim is not to develop musical skill. Rather, he or shet encourages clients to express themselves by trying out instruments, improvising together, establishing trust, building confidence and having fun through sound.

Training and skills

To work as a state-registered music therapist you will generally need to complete a three-year degree course or diploma in music, followed by a postgraduate course in music therapy. This will include work placements in settings such as hospitals and schools. Music therapists often work closely with other professionals such as doctors, psychologists and speech therapists, and you will be expected to have strong communication skills and work well in a team.

Any questions

What is a peripatetic teacher?

A peripatetic teacher is someone who does not work in one place but travels round from one site to another. Some education authorities employ peripatetic teachers who specialise in a particular instrument, such as the violin, to teach small groups of pupils in a number of schools. Therapists are also used in this way, taking their skills to a variety of clinics, nursing homes and hospices on a regular basis.

Reaching an audience

It is perfectly possible to make music and not share it with anyone. However, most musicians agree on one thing. They want people to hear their music. Reaching this audience is what the music industry is all about.

Doing it live

There's nothing like a live performance. Long before the first CD is pressed, the first record deal signed, the first world tour announced, musicians have honed their skills in front of an audience of real people who are ready to listen, applaud, dance or, sometimes, walk out.

When musicians are starting out they usually have to organise their own gigs, book their own venues and sell their own tickets. This is all part of the musician's journey. And if you are not a musician yourself then learning how to do these things will give you vital experience if you want to work in the music industry.

Put on an event

The best way to reach an audience is to organise a gig, or, if DJ-ing is your thing, put on a club night. If you aren't a musician yourself, offer your services to a friend's band. You'll need to find and book a venue such as a school hall or

THINKING AHEAD

Promote it!

Find a strong, catchy name for your event. Make posters and leaflets and rope in everyone you can to spread the word.

• Work out a suitable price for tickets (don't forget to include the cost of hiring the venue and any equipment in your calculations) and ask for permission to sell them at your school or youth group.

• If you don't have any expenses such as venue hire then you might want to think about giving out tickets for free. What matters most is that people come!

youth club, decide on a programme, promote the event, make and sell tickets and make sure all the musicians get there on time!

Don't forget to obtain permission from the venue for anything you want to do (such as how late you'd like the gig to finish), and make sure that all the equipment you'll need is in place in advance. There's a lot to think about, but you'll be gaining the kind of experience that future employers in the music business take very seriously.

Get permission

Does your band perform cover versions? Remember that other people's music is protected by copyright. This means that it cannot be performed without permission. Every live music venue must have a Performing Rights Society (PRS) licence and is responsible for providing the PRS with details of any songs performed there.

Any questions ?

What is the most difficult thing about putting on an event?

Ben Ward, former promoter of local bands and now Director of the Tower Arts Centre in Winchester, UK, says: 'Every job has its difficulties. This business is based around getting people through the door and unfortunately that's the only measure of success. You can have a great show, put a lot of work in and really enjoy it but if no one comes to see the act then it's all been for nothing.'

← *If you want to put on a concert or a gig, get your friends involved with ticket sales and publicity.*

Live music promotions

Some people build entire careers out of putting on live concerts and music festivals. Promoters, bookers and event managers all get involved. The job opportunities are varied and exciting but the hours are long, the work is stressful and the competition is intense!

Different jobs

A promoter for a live music venue is someone who finds and books the right bands and musicians for a specific concert or an entire season of events.

He or she will organise contracts and arrange entertainment licences as well as the appropriate marketing and publicity. Other promoters might work on behalf of specific bands and musicians. Their job is to get them booked to perform at

↓ *Michael Eavis (centre) has organised and promoted one of the world's biggest and most famous music festivals at Glastonbury for the last 40 years. He says: 'I liked pop music and people so it seemed like a good idea to put the two together. It was all quite naïve when we started – we really hadn't a clue.'*

a venue, concert or music festival. Promoters also act as talent scouts, looking for new acts and then matching them with suitable events. They may also arrange concerts and live appearances, aiming to showcase the work of new bands or individual performers.

An event manager is responsible for coordinating a specific event such as a concert or festival. He or she will liaise with bookers, acts and promoters to make sure that everything runs smoothly.

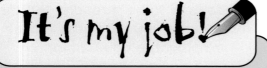

It's my job!

Alex Martin of Curious Generation, a music promotions company

"I arrive at the office between 8.30 and 9 am and get through a wad of emails from acts and booking agencies. I'll liaise with our event management team and look at the programme of events that are coming up. The afternoon is usually spent hosting meetings and keeping up with clients. At 8pm I'll head off to watch our gigs or check out new acts."

Necessary skills

Being a live music promoter requires energy, excellent organisation, a sound knowledge of music and business, the ability to recognise talent and great networking skills. Talking to people and building contacts is a vital part of the job.

There are music management courses available that can help you to develop business skills, but many people working in this area will have gained invaluable experience by promoting bands for free.

On the road

Technicians or 'roadies' set up instruments and other equipment before an outdoor gig.

When musicians tour or travel between venues, they need all kinds of help. An orchestra or band or a solo artist performing in a major arena must rely on 'roadies' – drivers, technicians, engineers, security staff and managers – who travel with them as part of the team.

THINKING AHEAD

You don't need any formal qualifications to be a roadie, but the more skills you have, the more employable you will be.

• Having a driving licence, especially a Large Goods Vehicle licence or Passenger Service Vehicle licence, will give you a definite advantage.

• For some more technical jobs you will need to demonstrate specific skills in electrics, sound production or lighting.

• It is a good idea to have taken a short health and safety course too.

A long day

The roadies are the first up in the morning, unloading and setting up equipment and preparing for sound checks. They also tend to be the last to finish at night as everything has to be packed away after the performance.

Most roadies are paid a day rate. They don't have the security of permanent employment but it can be a great way to participate in live performance and develop a specialist skill such as lighting or rigging.

Specialised work

When bands and artists are first starting out, everyone, including the musicians, tends to share the roadies' tasks. However, success usually means larger, better-known venues and bigger performances. The jobs become more specialised. Some really big acts assign a technician to each type of instrument, for example, to take responsibility for it, tune it and make sure it is in place when the musician needs it.

The sound engineer

Sound engineers operate equipment such as microphones and amplifiers, provide sound effects and balance sound levels. They will conduct sound checks with the musicians before a performance and operate the sound desk during live shows. Previous experience counts more than formal qualifications, and many sound engineers get their first gigs by working for free.

The tour manager

A successful tour manager will be on the road for eight or nine months a year, working three shows and then having a day off. There's a huge amount of preparation to see to, talking to agents and promoters, managing a crew of up to 100 people, booking the tour buses, flights and hotel rooms and coping with last-minute emergencies such as when a musician becomes ill or a flight is suddenly cancelled.

←
The sound engineer operates the sound desk during a live gig.

Recorded music

Live performance is one way to reach an audience, but if musicians want to make a lasting impact they need to record their music and find a way to market it and distribute it.

The record company

For decades the recorded music industry has been dominated by companies known as record labels. The record labels have traditionally 'discovered' the artists, produced the recordings and managed the marketing and distribution of the music. Despite the increasing competition from digital media they continue to employ thousands of people to find and develop new talent, arrange contracts and royalty payments, produce the music in the recording studio, organise the artwork and printing for the CD, promote the finished product in the media and arrange for digital content to be made available through a licensed online provider.

← A general admin job can be a good first step towards a career in a record company. As you become more experienced there may be opportunities to apply for jobs in departments such as promotions or A&R (see page 18).

The independent label

Smaller labels known as 'independents' or 'indie' labels are usually set up by people dedicated to producing and promoting a particular style of music. Often these independent labels struggle to make much money, but they are a great way to gain work experience. Being part of a small team means that each person is involved in every aspect of the business.

Digital downloads

Musicians and bands are increasingly beginning to take control of the production and distribution of their music, recording a CD themselves and making it available as a download. But a lot of downloading takes place illegally, without the artist's permission and without any payment to the artist. If you decide to get involved in the distribution of music via digital media, make sure that what you are doing is legal.

THINKING AHEAD

Record companies expect young people applying for a job to show commitment and knowledge about the music industry. Michael Pye, director of Human Resources at Universal Music UK, often interviews people for entry-level jobs. He says that while academic performance is important, experience is what really counts: 'It's a very creative industry and terribly hands-on. Even at the highest levels everyone is involved in the day-to-day business of signing artists and selling music. We like to feel that a new recruit can hit the ground running.'

It's my job!

Jo D'Andrea: owner and director of Jeepster Recordings Ltd.

"Working in an independent record company can be very rewarding because you work on a project from beginning to end rather than working in just one area. You get to work very closely with the artists and you also have greater control over what you do as a label. The difficulties come from not having any financial backing other than your own personal finances – this can sometimes be stressful for everyone."

Artist and Repertoire

Every time a record company invests in a new singer or band, they take a financial risk. Will the artist be worth the investment? The business of discovering new talent, getting a contract signed and then developing a sound that is both original and profitable for the record company is known as A&R, or Artist and Repertoire.

⬆ The members of London-based rock band Infadels celebrate signing their record deal with the Wall of Sound record label. Since signing the band has toured the UK and Europe and supported acts such as the Scissor Sisters.

Getting signed

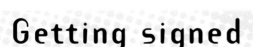

The A&R representative, or rep, is paid by the record company to build contacts in the industry, go to gigs, listen to demo packages (see page 13) and scout out new talent. Once the A&R reps find a musician or band that they like and think will make money for the record company, their job is to guide them through the process of agreeing a contract. This can involve lengthy negotiations over royalties, tour and promotional obligations and the sale of merchandise such as T-shirts.

Finding the right sound

A&R isn't just about getting signed, however. It also involves teaming the artists with the right music, choosing the right producer for the chosen sound, setting a recording budget and even overseeing promotional activities such as interviews with TV and press once the recording is complete.

Building a career

Many people view A&R as one of the most glamorous jobs in the music industry. However, getting paid to do it isn't easy. Many top A&R people have built up the necessary contacts and experience by being in a band themselves, or by DJ-ing or reviewing gigs or promoting bands for free. You'll have to demonstrate a sound insider's knowledge of a particular music scene before a record company will trust you to find and develop new artists.

It's my job!

Alec Boateng, A&R rep for Ministry of Sound

"My role requires me to look for new talent/projects. Then once the artist is signed, preparing the product and introducing it to the marketplace. I have the usual GCSEs, A Levels and a Marketing and Management degree but all the while I was DJing."

Any questions

Why do some bands prefer not to sign a contract with a record company?

'Record companies are a kind of army – very regulated,' says Alan McGee, founder of Creation Records and former manager of The Charlatans. 'Whilst live music and merchandise sales are booming, physical [CD] sales are steadily decreasing with more and more fans simply burning tracks from friends or free download sites. The band will get paid more by more people coming to the gigs, buying merchandise and other fees. I believe it is the future business model.'

← *Ollie Cooper of indie band Koopa – the first unsigned band to enter the UK Top 40 through downloads alone. They have since signed a contract with a record company.*

In the studio

The recording studio is where music is recorded and mixed before being transferred to CD or digital media. Some record companies have their own studios, while other studios are available for hire by musicians or record companies. However, it is perfectly possible to set up the necessary equipment in a bedroom or a garage and do it yourself!

Recording and mixing

Each voice or instrument is recorded separately in the studio, so it can be a time-consuming process if the music involves lots of different elements. Then the individual sounds are carefully 'mixed' and balanced to create the finished piece of music, or 'master' track.

Sound recording engineer Mike Ross-Trevor at work on a mixing desk at the Sony studios in London. The instruments of the orchestra are recorded separately before they are mixed to create the finished sound.

The music producer

Music producers control the recording sessions, guide the performers and supervise the mixing process. They need to have a clear idea of what kind of sound they want to achieve as well as having technical skills.

Some music producers may work 'in-house' for a studio or a record company, but many work freelance and are brought in by a record company or an artist or band because of their skill in creating a particular type of sound.

Studio engineers

Studio engineers set up and test the recording equipment, monitor sound levels and often assist at the mixing desk. They work alongside the producer, using their knowledge of the technology to create the best sounds and specific effects. The job requires considerable technical knowledge, and some engineers will have taken a music technology course. However others learn on the job, working as an assistant or 'runner' in a recording studio.

Any questions?

I'm interested in producing music for computer games. How can I do this?

Music for computer games, websites, TV commercials and corporate videos requires the skills of a producer who understands how music relates to the image on the screen. One way to develop skills and experience is to record and mix sounds on some home studio equipment, pairing them with video footage or computer animation to see what works and what doesn't. If the images are free from copyright then you can post your finished piece on a video-sharing website and ask for feedback.

← A studio engineer works with Malverde, a hip-hop artist, as he rehearses in a recording studio in Hollywood in the United States.

Selling the sound

The sale of recorded music is big business in the UK. In 2007, revenue from recorded music was just over £1 billion, making the UK the third biggest market in the world. This means a wide range of job opportunities in retail and digital download companies.

CD sales

Despite the fact that sales of CDs are falling each year, largely due to the increase in music downloads from the internet, music stores and other retailers continue to sell CDs in significant quantities. Getting a job in a music store isn't just a great way to get paid to listen to music all day. It also helps you learn about music trends, gain valuable retail experience and understand how music marketing works.

It's my job!

Jill Thomas, HMV Marketing Manager for Ireland

"I started to work in HMV as a Christmas temp ten years ago. I've always loved music and it seemed like the perfect way to combine my main interests with work. Then, after graduating from university, I was lucky enough to be given a place on HMV's graduate trainee programme... My current position involves looking after the marketing across Ireland. I also coordinate in-store events such as personal appearances – when artists and bands visit to meet fans and to perform live or sign copies of their latest releases and look after sponsorship opportunities. There's always something different to do and so many great people to meet – it keeps me highly motivated."

← *Working in music retail sales is a great way to gain experience and meet customers face-to-face.*

Digital sales

More and more people are buying the music they want through digital downloads. However, despite the rapid growth of digital music sales, careers in this area are still relatively scarce and employees work within a small organisational structure. Entry-level jobs include personal assistants, marketing assistants, web developers and customer services officers.

Employees need to demonstrate a commitment to music, an understanding of digital media and an outgoing, adaptable personality – someone who welcomes rapid developments in the technology.

Merchandise

Selling the sound is about more than the music sales themselves. Increasingly, bands and record companies are looking to sales of associated merchandise such as T-shirts, posters and dvds to promote their brand and increase their profits.

Merchandise is sold at gigs, online and through shops and stores and if you want to gain experience selling your own music merchandise, take a look at websites such as www.overplay.co.uk which offer an online 'shop window' for a fee.

↑ It's important to pay for the music you download. Illegal downloads take income away from those working in the music industry, from the artists themselves to the people who clean the recording studios.

THINKING AHEAD

A degree in marketing proved invaluable for Leanne Sharman, former Vice President and UK General Manager for Napster. She says 'It was a very practical course and I learned about subjects like business law, accountancy and marketing.' However, she says an impressive CV isn't just about qualifications. Proving a commitment to music through experience working at a music venue or managing a friend's band is just as important. 'If I meet someone with the enthusiasm to say "I can see the potential of digital music and I really want to be part of this company," then that's great. I'm looking for that passion when I recruit.'

Music and the media

There are two sides to music and the media. On the one side are those making, marketing and selling music – these people want to promote and play their music through the media. On the other side are those working in radio, television, magazines and newspapers or even writing online blogs – their job is to find out about music and bring it to their listeners, viewers and readers.

↑ *People who work in public relations spend a lot of time on the phone and in meetings, so they need excellent 'people skills' to do their job well.*

Public Relations (PR)

Artists, record companies and retailers all want to get people listening to their music by promoting it through the media. The PR department of a record company, for example, will send out press releases to all relevant media to inform them about a new artist or a new album release. They will organise public appearances and invite journalists to interview their artists, often personally accompanying them from one location to another. They will also try to persuade radio and TV shows to play a particular CD – this is known as 'plugging'.

Daniel Lloyd Jones

Daniel Lloyd Jones now runs his own press company and works for EMI Music Publishing. His first job was as a press assistant at Warners. He says 'In 2004 I was made junior press officer and given My Chemical Romance to look after. No one really knew who they were then; they were just a little Emo outfit from New Jersey. I got them their first Kerrang! cover and they went on to become massive.'

Communication skills

To be successful in PR you'll need to have great communication skills in order to build and maintain contacts in the media. You'll also need to be diplomatic, meeting the requirements of your employer while recognising the pressures faced by journalists, DJs and editors. A good telephone manner and excellent writing skills are essential. An ability to spot new media opportunities will help, too!

Work placements

Some record companies offer work placement schemes in their PR departments. Usually this involves answering phones, photocopying press releases and acting as an assistant, or runner in the office. The work will almost certainly be unpaid, but it is a fantastic way to find out about PR and the music media.

THINKING AHEAD

Sarah Hand, resourcing officer at Universal Music UK says: 'We look for experience such as work placements at a record label or doing music writing for the student newspaper. Something that shows someone is passionate about music, that it's part of their life and that they have some understanding of how the industry works.'

← The members of Take That face journalists, photographers and TV crews at a press conference in November 2005 as they announce that the band is reforming. Organising press conferences is an important apect of a job in PR.

Working in radio

One of the best things about radio is the enormous variety of shows and stations dedicated to particular kinds of music. Whether your interests are classical, country, world music or indie, a job in radio enables you to work in a fast-moving environment, surrounded by the music you love!

The producer

Radio producers work for a specific programme or show. Their role is to manage the show from behind the scenes, helping to select the music, talking to 'pluggers' from record companies, controlling the running order, booking interviews with guests and supporting (and sometimes training) the presenter. It isn't all about the live broadcast, though. There's paperwork to do, and the day usually starts and ends in the office.

The presenter

The presenter or DJ hosts the show, introducing the music on air, talking to guests and often controlling the cues for clips, jingles and pre-recorded interviews.

↑ *Recording artist Lemar congratulates DJ Jon Scragg at the launch of radio station Smooth FM. Different radio stations cater for a range of musical tastes.*

The job demands excellent communication skills, a clear speaking voice, the ability to remain calm and cheerful under intense pressure as well as a passion for music that the audience can connect with.

A national radio show will have a big team of producers, broadcast assistants and editors to support the presenter and prepare sequences in advance, but smaller stations require the presenter to do several jobs at the same time – often acting as producer and editor as well as DJ.

The runner

Runners are general assistants whose job can involve anything from sorting the post, fetching coffee, logging music as it comes into the office, ordering stationery, issuing passes to guests and staff and helping to sort out problems as they occur. It's a great entry – level job as you'll get to see how radio works as well as meet guests and listen to new music before anyone else does.

Some radio stations offer work experience but competition is huge so you'll need to demonstrate your knowledge and commitment as well as good organisational skills if you want that place.

↓ *Working in radio sometimes involves helping out at outside broadcasts or 'roadshows' as well as being based in a studio.*

It's my job!

Chiara, runner at Radio 1

"I studied music at school and then did a **BTEC National Diploma** in Media. After the course finished I approached a house and garage label called Pure Silk for work experience. After three weeks there they asked me to work full time as a runner. A year later, I heard about the job at Radio 1, applied and got it."

Any questions?

Do you have to be really pushy to get a job in radio?

No one wants the hassle of working with someone who doesn't know when to back off or keep quiet. However, you do need to be confident and determined if you want to get noticed. You'll have to call people who don't know you and persuade them to take you on but most employers don't mind this just as long as you are polite. Being polite doesn't mean you can't be persistent – remember that employers are looking for people who are good communicators, work hard and can operate as part of a team.

Music journalism

If you love music and you love writing about it, music journalism may be the career for you. There are lots of ways you can do this: work for a magazine or newspaper, create a fanzine, write reviews or start your own online music blog.

News, reviews and interviews

Newspaper and magazine editors expect the journalists they hire to be experienced writers. So how does an aspiring music journalist get experience?

The answer is, by going to gigs and concerts, interviewing artists and writing reviews they can post online or send out to some of the smaller publications or a particular type of music.

Try reviewing your friends' music, or a CD that has just been released. Be honest and aim to give your writing a distinctive voice or tone. Develop a critical approach by reading the work of other music journalists. Look online and in newspapers and magazines.

←

A reporter from Rolling Stone music magazine in the United States interviews band members from Taking Back Sunday, My Chemical Romance and Linkin Park as they announce a tour in 2007. Filming an interview is a good way of keeping a record of what has been said.

Building a career

Most music journalists work freelance, so building a reputation for a certain writing style or coverage of a particular kind of music will help your writing to stand out from the crowd.

If you want to get a permanent job with a magazine or fanzine make sure you've got good typing and computer skills and be prepared to work as the office junior for a while. This will help you gain the experience to take on jobs such as editorial assistant, with some writing responsibilities. Once you have been published, keep all your clippings – they will be your passport to more work.

Get blogging

A blog is another name for an online diary or web journal. For many, blogging is a form of instant publication. There is no faster way to reach your potential audience. Whether you want to hone your writing skills and get noticed as a music journalist, or simply want to take part in an ongoing conversation about the kind of music you love, the blog is increasingly becoming the medium of choice for many people across the music business.

Any questions

I want to write for a major music magazine. What qualifications will I need?

Some editors will expect you to have an NCTJ qualification from the National Council for the Training of Journalists. However, a sample of your writing as well as some original ideas for features is more likely to get you noticed. It is important to remember that editors need writers who can deliver their work on time, with the right amount of words, in a style appropriate for their publication.

THINKING AHEAD

Tips for blogging:
- Register on www.blogger.com or a similar blog host (tell a responsible adult what you are doing).
- Give your blog a catchy name and a clear focus. What kind of music are you writing about, and why?
- Aim for a distinctive voice or tone – try writing as if you are talking to someone.
- Update regularly – daily is good.
- Avoid bad language, don't copy someone else's work and don't say anything you might regret later.
- Tell all your family and friends to read it and spread the word!

Glossary

A&R or 'Artist and Repertoire' people employed by a record company to discover and develop new artists and match them with the right music

blogging publishing your views, opinions and reviews online

booker sometimes known as a booking agent; arranges for an artist or band to appear at a live concert or gig

chamber music a form of classical music written for a small number of instruments

conservatoire a school or college for the study and performance of classical music

copyright a form of legal protection for artists that prevents anyone from copying or using their work without their permission

degree a university-level qualification

demo package a tool for getting your music noticed; consists of a CD of your music, photos of you, any press cuttings and a few biographical details

digital media a way of delivering material such as music through digital tools such as the internet (music downloads, for example)

diploma a type of qualification

distribute to make available; for example getting CDs into the shops

fanzine a magazine for fans of a particular artist or band

marketed getting a product noticed and sold

mixing merging sounds recorded separately to produce a finished recording

music therapist someone who uses music to help clients deal with a range of problems

networking building contacts through meeting people

plugging trying to get a particular music track played on radio or TV

postgraduate a higher degree taken after a first university degree

press officer someone who deals with the media on behalf of an artist or a company

press release a statement issued to the media, giving information about a new product or artist

producer the person who controls the recording process in the studio

promoter someone who matches artists with the right gigs and events

PRS licence permission from the Performing Rights Society to perform someone else's work

record label the record company; large record companies may have different labels for different types of music

roadie a person who travels with an artist or band while they are on tour; technical crew, drivers and security staff are all 'roadies'

royalty an artist's earnings from CD sales or from the use of their music by advertisers, film makers and so on

runner an assistant working for a radio station

running order the sequence or order in which different music tracks are played

scout a talent spotter

self-employed working for yourself

sound check a test carried out before a gig or a recording to make sure that all the equipment is working properly

sound desk the technical controls operated by a sound engineer

sound engineer a technician who helps the musicians achieve the best sounds

tour manager the person who makes all the arrangements for a tour and sorts out any problems during the tour

web developer someone who designs new website applications

work placement a short period of work experience, often unpaid, with a specific company

Further information

The Creative and Media Diploma

The Diploma is a qualification for 14 to 19 year-olds which combines classroom-based study with practical hands-on work experience. It enables you to find out more about the careers you're interested in without having to commit to one of them. Find out more information about the Creative and Media Diploma at:
http://yp.direct.gov.uk/diplomas/subjects/Creative_Media/index.cfm

Book

People at Work: Creative and Media by Jan Champney (Franklin Watts, 2008)

Websites

www.makeyourmark.org.uk/get_involved/make_your_mark_in_music
This is the website for the 'Make Your Mark in the Music Business' campaign. It contains a range of inspiring stories from people producing and selling music.

www.bbc.co.uk/radio1/onemusic/workr1
The Radio 1 website contains lots of detailed job profiles along with practical advice on applying for work experience placements.

www.youngenterprise.org.uk/qsmusic/home.htm
If you are aged between 13 and 15 this site will explain how you can set up and run your own music enterprise scheme at school, putting on a music event or producing and selling a music product.

www.overplay.co.uk
This is a commercial site designed to give unsigned artists a platform to be seen and heard and sell their music online. Great for seeing how other people do it!

www.careersinmusic.co.uk
This site is full of relevant, practical information and advice for anyone seeking a career in the music business. It gives useful addresses, job profiles and valuable 'workshops' on setting up a home studio, recording and mixing sounds and so on.

www.bbc.co.uk/music/parents/careersguide/index.shtml
Designed for parents who want to know more about music-related career options, this site is equally useful for young people. Jobs are presented with a realistic overview from industry professionals.

www.nhscareers.nhs.uk/details/Default.aspx?Id=432
Clear information about the principles of music therapy and the variety of work carried out by music therapists.

Index

Numbers in **bold** refer to pictures.

Behind the Scenes

Contents of titles in the series:

WAYLAND